Revive & Thrive

A 90-Day Journey to Reignite Your Marriage

Dr. Tomeka Lynch Purcell

Revive & Thrive: A 90-Day Journey to Reignite Your Marriage

Please direct all copyright inquiries to:

B.O.Y. Publications, Inc.
c/o Author Copyrights
P.O. Box 262
Lowell, NC 28098
betonyourselfent.com

Paperback ISBN: 978-1-955605-80-9

Cover and Interior Design: B.O.Y. Enterprises, Inc.

Printed in the United States.

DEDICATION

To every couple who picks up this journal, may your
marriage be forever changed for the better!
It's time to Revive & Thrive!

Building Self-Esteem

Building Self-Esteem

Day 1

Date: _____

Write affirmations for each other and read them together every morning.

Husband's Affirmations for His Wife:

_____

_____

_____

_____

_____

_____

Wife's Affirmations for Her Husband:

_____

_____

_____

_____

_____

_____

_____

Building Self-Esteem

Day 2

Date: _____

Write affirmations for each other and read them together every morning.

Husband's Affirmations for His Wife:

_____
_____
_____
_____
_____
_____

Wife's Affirmations for Her Husband:

_____
_____
_____
_____
_____
_____

Building Self-Esteem

Day 3

Date: _____

Write affirmations for each other and read them together
every morning.

Husband's Affirmations for His Wife:

_____
_____
_____
_____
_____
_____

Wife's Affirmations for Her Husband:

_____
_____
_____
_____
_____
_____

Building Self-Esteem

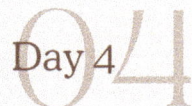

Day 4

Date: _____

Write affirmations for each other and read them together every morning.

Husband's Affirmations for His Wife:

_____

_____

_____

_____

_____

Wife's Affirmations for Her Husband:

_____

_____

_____

_____

_____

Building Self-Esteem

Day 5 05

Date: _____

Write affirmations for each other and read them together every morning.

Husband's Affirmations for His Wife:

_____

_____

_____

_____

_____

_____

Wife's Affirmations for Her Husband:

_____

_____

_____

_____

_____

_____

_____

Building Self-Esteem

Day 6

Date: _____

Devote 15 minutes to individual personal development daily.

> ### Wife's Personal Development Activity

_____
_____
_____
_____
_____
_____

> ### Husband's Personal Development Activity

_____
_____
_____
_____
_____
_____

Building Self-Esteem

Day 7

Date: _____

Devote 15 minutes to individual personal development daily.

Wife's Personal Development Activity

_____

_____

_____

_____

_____

Husband's Personal Development Activity

_____

_____

_____

_____

_____

_____

Building Self-Esteem

 Day 8

Date: _____

Devote 15 minutes to individual personal development daily.

Wife's Personal Development Activity

_____
_____
_____
_____
_____
_____

Husband's Personal Development Activity

_____
_____
_____
_____
_____
_____

Building Self-Esteem

Day 9

Date: _____

Devote 15 minutes to individual personal development daily.

Wife's Personal Development Activity

_____
_____
_____
_____
_____

Husband's Personal Development Activity

_____
_____
_____
_____
_____
_____

Building Self-Esteem

10

Day 10

Date: _____

Devote 15 minutes to individual personal development daily.

> ### Wife's Personal Development Activity

_____

_____

_____

_____

_____

_____

> ### Husband's Personal Development Activity

_____

_____

_____

_____

_____

Building Self-Esteem

Day 11   Date:_____

Engage in an activity or hobby that boosts confidence. In the space below, list the activity you completed and how you felt afterwards.

Husband

_____
_____
_____
_____
_____
_____

Wife

_____
_____
_____
_____
_____
_____

Building Self-Esteem

Day 12

Date: _____

Engage in an activity or hobby that boosts confidence. In the space below, list the activity you completed and how you felt afterwards.

Husband

_____
_____
_____
_____
_____
_____

Wife

_____
_____
_____
_____
_____
_____

Building Self-Esteem

Day 13

Date: _____

Engage in an activity or hobby that boosts confidence. In the space below, list the activity you completed and how you felt afterwards.

Husband

_____
_____
_____
_____
_____
_____

Wife

_____
_____
_____
_____
_____
_____

Building Self-Esteem

Day 14

Date: _____

Engage in an activity or hobby that boosts confidence. In the space below, list the activity you completed and how you felt afterwards.

Husband

_____
_____
_____
_____
_____
_____

Wife

_____
_____
_____
_____
_____
_____

Building Self-Esteem

Date: _____

Engage in an activity or hobby that boosts confidence. In the space below, list the activity you completed and how you felt afterwards.

Husband

_____
_____
_____
_____
_____
_____

Wife

_____
_____
_____
_____
_____
_____

Building Self-Esteem

Day  16

Date: _____

Share past struggles and discuss growth and learning. Use the space below to write the struggle, then share what you wrote with your spouse.

Husband

_____
_____
_____
_____
_____

Wife

_____
_____
_____
_____
_____

Building Self-Esteem

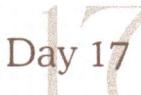

Day 17

Share past struggles and discuss growth and learning. Use the space below to write the struggle, then share what you wrote with your spouse.

Husband

_____
_____
_____
_____
_____
_____

Wife

_____
_____
_____
_____
_____
_____

Building Self-Esteem

Day 18

Date: _____

Share past struggles and discuss growth and learning. Use the space below to write the struggle, then share what you wrote with your spouse.

Husband

_____
_____
_____
_____
_____

Wife

_____
_____
_____
_____
_____

Building Self-Esteem

Day 19

Date: _____

Share past struggles and discuss growth and learning. Use the space below to write the struggle, then share what you wrote with your spouse.

Husband

_____
_____
_____
_____
_____
_____

Wife

_____
_____
_____
_____
_____
_____

Building Self-Esteem

Day 20

Date: _____

Share past struggles and discuss growth and learning. Use the space below to write the struggle, then share what you wrote with your spouse.

Husband

_____
_____
_____
_____
_____

Wife

_____
_____
_____
_____
_____

Building Self-Esteem

Day 21

Date: _____

Small style updates can go a long way towards improving confidence and self-esteem. For the next five days, focus on personal grooming or style updates. List the style update you chose below.

Husband

_____

_____

_____

_____

Wife

_____

_____

_____

_____

Building Self-Esteem

Day 22

Date: _____

Small style updates can go a long way towards improving confidence and self-esteem. For the next five days, focus on personal grooming or style updates. List the style update you chose below.

Husband

_____
_____
_____
_____

Wife

_____
_____
_____
_____

Building Self-Esteem

Day 23

Date: _____

Small style updates can go a long way towards improving confidence and self-esteem. For the next five days, focus on personal grooming or style updates. List the style update you chose below.

Husband

_____
_____
_____
_____

Wife

_____
_____
_____
_____

Building Self-Esteem

Day 24

Date: _____

Small style updates can go a long way towards improving confidence and self-esteem. For the next five days, focus on personal grooming or style updates. List the style update you chose below.

Husband

_____

_____

_____

Wife

_____

_____

_____

_____

Building Self-Esteem

Day 25

Date: _____

Small style updates can go a long way towards improving confidence and self-esteem. For the next five days, focus on personal grooming or style updates. List the style update you chose below.

Husband

_____

_____

_____

_____

Wife

_____

_____

_____

_____

Building Self-Esteem

Date: _____

For the next five days, you're going to celebrate your accomplishments together. Each night, write an accomplishment below, then share it with your spouse and spend a few minutes verbally celebrate each other's wins.

Husband

_____

_____

_____

_____

Wife

_____

_____

_____

_____

Building Self-Esteem

Date: _____

For the next five days, you're going to celebrate your accomplishments together. Each night, write an accomplishment below, then share it with your spouse and spend a few minutes verbally celebrate each other's wins.

Husband

_____
_____
_____
_____

Wife

_____
_____
_____
_____

Building Self-Esteem

Day 28

Date: _____

For the next five days, you're going to celebrate your accomplishments together. Each night, write an accomplishment below, then share it with your spouse and spend a few minutes verbally celebrate each other's wins.

Husband

_____
_____
_____
_____

Wife

_____
_____
_____
_____

Building Self-Esteem

Date: _____

For the next five days, you're going to celebrate your accomplishments together. Each night, write an accomplishment below, then share it with your spouse and spend a few minutes verbally celebrate each other's wins.

Husband

_____

_____

_____

_____

Wife

_____

_____

_____

_____

Building Self-Esteem

Date: _____

For the next five days, you're going to celebrate your accomplishments together. Each night, write an accomplishment below, then share it with your spouse and spend a few minutes verbally celebrate each other's wins.

Husband

_____
_____
_____
_____

Wife

_____
_____
_____
_____

Cultivating Intimacy

Cultivating Intimacy

Day 31

Date: _____

Designate tech-free time for daily intimate conversations. In the
space below, write down the topics you discussed during your

Intimate
Conversation Topics

1. _____
2. _____
3. _____
4. _____
5. _____

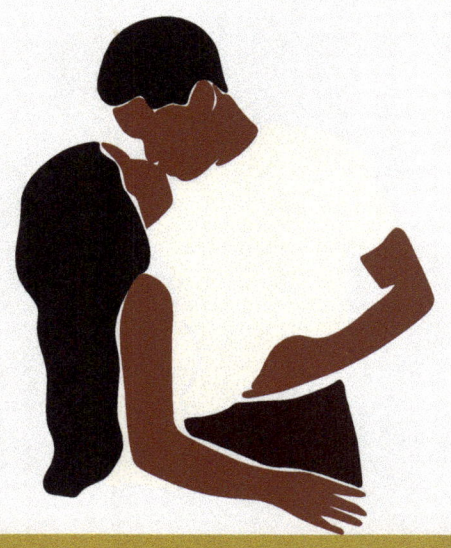

Cultivating Intimacy

Day 32

Date: _____

Designate tech-free time for daily intimate conversations. In the space below, write down the topics you discussed during your

Intimate Conversation Topics

1. _____

2. _____

3. _____

4. _____

5. _____

Cultivating Intimacy

Day 33

Date: _____

Designate tech-free time for daily intimate conversations. In the space below, write down the topics you discussed during your

Intimate Conversation Topics

1. _____
2. _____
3. _____
4. _____
5. _____

Cultivating Intimacy

Day 34

Date: _____

Designate tech-free time for daily intimate conversations. In the space below, write down the topics you discussed during your

Intimate Conversation Topics

1. _____
2. _____
3. _____
4. _____
5. _____

Cultivating Intimacy

Day 35

Date: _____

Designate tech-free time for daily intimate conversations. In the space below, write down the topics you discussed during your

Intimate Conversation Topics

1. _____
2. _____
3. _____
4. _____
5. _____

Cultivating Intimacy

Days 36-40 – 40

Date: _____

Rediscover Flirting
Intimacy begins long before you touch each
other's bodies. For the next five days, send each
other sweet or cheeky notes.

(P.S. There are lines below, but you can just write down
the text messages you are comfortable recording. In
other words, if you have nosey children who aren't
ready to know how Mommy and Daddy really get
down... leave the space below blank.)

_____

_____

_____

_____

_____

_____

Cultivating Intimacy

Days 41-45

Date: _____

In the space below, plan 15 unique date nights (3 per day). These can be intimate nights at home, trips to your favorite places, or new local eateries and/or attractions you'd like to try. Sit down with your spouse and plan these together to boost intimacy and spark excitement about the dates to come. Happy planning!

1. _____
2. _____
3. _____
4. _____
5. _____
6. _____
7. _____
8. _____
9. _____
10. _____
11. _____
12. _____
13. _____
14. _____
15. _____

Cultivating Intimacy

Days 46-50

Date: _____

Share a favorite book or movie, and discuss themes and ideas afterward. Write the titles of the books and/or movies you discussed below.

DAY 46: _____

DAY 47: _____

DAY 48: _____

DAY 49: _____

DAY 50: _____

What did you discover about one another during these discussions?

Cultivating Intimacy

51-55

Days 51-55

Date: _____

Spend the next five days focusing on physical affection. Hold hands, hug longer, give each other a few extra kisses, or cuddle as you relax in each other's arms.

Love is not finding someone to live with, it's finding someone you can't live without.

Cultivating Intimacy

Day 56

Date: _____

Write intimate and honest love letters and exchange them.

> *Husband's Letter to Wife*

_____

_____

_____

_____

_____

_____

_____

_____

_____

_____

_____

_____

_____

_____

_____

_____

_____

_____

_____

_____

•you & me•

Cultivating Intimacy

Day 56

Date: _____

Write intimate and honest love letters and exchange them.

Wife's Letter to Husband

_____

_____

_____

_____

_____

_____

_____

_____

_____

_____

_____

_____

_____

_____

_____

_____

_____

• you & me •

Cultivating Intimacy

Day 57

Date: _____

Write intimate and honest love letters and exchange them.

> *Husband's Letter to Wife*

_____

_____

_____

_____

_____

_____

_____

_____

_____

_____

_____

_____

_____

_____

_____

_____

_____

_____

_____

_____

• *you & me* •

Cultivating Intimacy

Day 57

Date: _____

Write intimate and honest love letters and exchange them.

> *Wife's Letter to Husband*

_____

_____

_____

_____

_____

_____

_____

_____

_____

_____

_____

_____

_____

_____

_____

_____

_____

_____

_____

Cultivating Intimacy

Day 58

Date: _____

Write intimate and honest love letters and exchange them.

Husband's Letter to Wife

_____

_____

_____

_____

_____

_____

_____

_____

_____

_____

_____

_____

_____

_____

_____

_____

_____

_____

_____

_____

• you & me •

Cultivating Intimacy

Day 58

Date: _____

Write intimate and honest love letters and exchange them.

> *Wife's Letter to Husband*

_____

_____

_____

_____

_____

_____

_____

_____

_____

_____

_____

_____

_____

_____

_____

• you & me •

Cultivating Intimacy

Day 59

Date: _____

Write intimate and honest love letters and exchange them.

> *Husband's Letter to Wife*

_____

_____

_____

_____

_____

_____

_____

_____

_____

_____

_____

_____

_____

_____

•you & me•

Cultivating Intimacy

Day 59

Date: _____

Write intimate and honest love letters and exchange them.

Wife's Letter to Husband

_____

_____

_____

_____

_____

_____

_____

_____

_____

_____

_____

_____

_____

_____

_____

_____

_____

Cultivating Intimacy

Day 60

Date: _____

Write intimate and honest love letters and exchange them.

> *Husband's Letter to Wife*

_____
_____
_____
_____
_____
_____
_____
_____
_____
_____
_____
_____
_____
_____
_____
_____
_____
_____

• you & me •

Cultivating Intimacy

Day 60

Date: _____

Write intimate and honest love letters and exchange them.

> *Wife's Letter to Husband*

_____

_____

_____

_____

_____

_____

_____

_____

_____

_____

_____

_____

_____

_____

_____

_____

Financial Harmony

Financial Harmony

Days 61-65

Date:_____

Sit together to review your current financial status and set a shared vision.

Our Vision for Our Finances

_____

_____

_____

_____

_____

_____

_____

_____

_____

_____

_____

_____

_____

_____

_____

_____

_____

MONTHLY INCOME *Tracker*

JANUARY
Total $

Notes

FEBRUARY
Total $

Notes

MARCH
Total $

Notes

APRIL
Total $

Notes

MAY
Total $

Notes

JUNE
Total $

Notes

JULY
Total $

Notes

AUGUST
Total $

Notes

SEPTEMBER
Total $

Notes

OCTOBER
Total $

Notes

NOVEMBER
Total $

Notes

DECEMBER
Total $

Notes

MONTHLY *expenses*

Month:_____

RECURRING EXPENSES	
Mortgage/Rent, Auto Loan/Lease, Insurance, etc...	Amount
_____	
_____	
_____	
_____	
_____	
_____	
_____	
_____	
_____	
_____	
TOTAL RECURRING EXPENSES	$

VARIABLE EXPENSES	
Utilities, Groceries, Maintenance Expenses, etc...	Amount
_____	
_____	
_____	
_____	
_____	
TOTAL VARIABLE EXPENSES	$

TOTAL MONTHLY EXPENSES	$

MONTHLY *expenses*

Month:_____

RECURRING EXPENSES

Mortgage/Rent, Auto Loan/Lease, Insurance, etc...	Amount
TOTAL RECURRING EXPENSES	$

VARIABLE EXPENSES

Utilities, Groceries, Maintenance Expenses, etc...	Amount
TOTAL VARIABLE EXPENSES	$

TOTAL MONTHLY EXPENSES | $

MONTHLY *expenses*

Month:_____

RECURRING EXPENSES	
Mortgage/Rent, Auto Loan/Lease, Insurance, etc...	Amount
TOTAL RECURRING EXPENSES	$

VARIABLE EXPENSES	
Utilities, Groceries, Maintenance Expenses, etc...	Amount
TOTAL VARIABLE EXPENSES	$

TOTAL MONTHLY EXPENSES	$

MONTHLY *expenses*

Month:_____

RECURRING EXPENSES	
Mortgage/Rent, Auto Loan/Lease, Insurance, etc...	Amount
_____	
_____	
_____	
_____	
_____	
_____	
_____	
_____	
_____	
_____	
TOTAL RECURRING EXPENSES	$

VARIABLE EXPENSES	
Utilities, Groceries, Maintenance Expenses, etc...	Amount
_____	
_____	
_____	
_____	
_____	
_____	
TOTAL VARIABLE EXPENSES	$

TOTAL MONTHLY EXPENSES	$

MONTHLY *expenses*

Month:_____

RECURRING EXPENSES	
Mortgage/Rent, Auto Loan/Lease, Insurance, etc...	Amount
TOTAL RECURRING EXPENSES	$

VARIABLE EXPENSES	
Utilities, Groceries, Maintenance Expenses, etc...	Amount
TOTAL VARIABLE EXPENSES	$

TOTAL MONTHLY EXPENSES	$

MONTHLY *expenses*

Month:_____

RECURRING EXPENSES	
Mortgage/Rent, Auto Loan/Lease, Insurance, etc...	Amount
TOTAL RECURRING EXPENSES	$

VARIABLE EXPENSES	
Utilities, Groceries, Maintenance Expenses, etc...	Amount
TOTAL VARIABLE EXPENSES	$

TOTAL MONTHLY EXPENSES	$

MONTHLY *expenses*

Month:_____

RECURRING EXPENSES	
Mortgage/Rent, Auto Loan/Lease, Insurance, etc...	Amount
TOTAL RECURRING EXPENSES	$

VARIABLE EXPENSES	
Utilities, Groceries, Maintenance Expenses, etc...	Amount
TOTAL VARIABLE EXPENSES	$

TOTAL MONTHLY EXPENSES	$

MONTHLY *expenses*

Month:_____

RECURRING EXPENSES	
Mortgage/Rent, Auto Loan/Lease, Insurance, etc...	Amount
TOTAL RECURRING EXPENSES	$

VARIABLE EXPENSES	
Utilities, Groceries, Maintenance Expenses, etc...	Amount
TOTAL VARIABLE EXPENSES	$

TOTAL MONTHLY EXPENSES	$

MONTHLY *expenses*

Month:_____

RECURRING EXPENSES	
Mortgage/Rent, Auto Loan/Lease, Insurance, etc...	Amount
TOTAL RECURRING EXPENSES	$

VARIABLE EXPENSES	
Utilities, Groceries, Maintenance Expenses, etc...	Amount
TOTAL VARIABLE EXPENSES	$

TOTAL MONTHLY EXPENSES	$

MONTHLY *expenses*

Month:_____

RECURRING EXPENSES

Mortgage/Rent, Auto Loan/Lease, Insurance, etc... | Amount

_____ |
_____ |
_____ |
_____ |
_____ |
_____ |
_____ |
_____ |
_____ |

TOTAL RECURRING EXPENSES | $

VARIABLE EXPENSES

Utilities, Groceries, Maintenance Expenses, etc... | Amount

_____ |
_____ |
_____ |
_____ |

TOTAL VARIABLE EXPENSES | $

TOTAL MONTHLY EXPENSES | $

MONTHLY *expenses*

Month:_____

RECURRING EXPENSES	
Mortgage/Rent, Auto Loan/Lease, Insurance, etc...	Amount
TOTAL RECURRING EXPENSES	$

VARIABLE EXPENSES	
Utilities, Groceries, Maintenance Expenses, etc...	Amount
TOTAL VARIABLE EXPENSES	$

TOTAL MONTHLY EXPENSES	$

MONTHLY *expenses*

Month:_____

RECURRING EXPENSES	
Mortgage/Rent, Auto Loan/Lease, Insurance, etc...	Amount
TOTAL RECURRING EXPENSES	$

VARIABLE EXPENSES	
Utilities, Groceries, Maintenance Expenses, etc...	Amount
TOTAL VARIABLE EXPENSES	$

TOTAL MONTHLY EXPENSES	$

Financial Harmony

Date: _____

Now that you've reviewed your income and expenses, and discussed your vision for your finances, spend the next 5 days creating a budget that allows you to save and still enjoy moments together.

Implement the budget you create for one month. If changes are needed, make adjustments using the additional budget template pages. Continue this process until you create a budget that works best for the financial vision you created together.

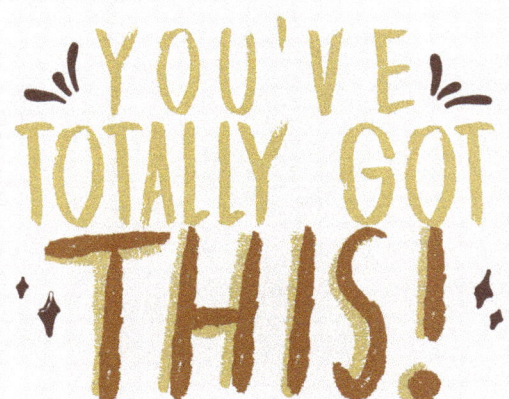

MONTHLY BUDGET

MONTH OF:

FIXED INCOME	
SIDE HUSTLE	
OTHER	
TOTAL INCOME	

CATEGORY	AMOUNT	AMOUNT USED	SAVED
RENT			
UTILITIES			
PHONE			
INSURANCE			
LOAN PAYMENTS			
GROCERIES			
DINING OUT			
TRANSPORTATION			
ENTERTAINMENT			
PERSONAL CARE			
HEALTH			
EMERGENCY FUND			
DONATIONS			
SUBSCRIPTIONS			
HOBBIES			
VACATIONS			
INVESTMENTS			

TOTAL INCOME	
TOTAL EXPENSES	
NET SAVINGS	

MONTHLY BUDGET

MONTH OF:

FIXED INCOME	
SIDE HUSTLE	
OTHER	
TOTAL INCOME	

CATEGORY	AMOUNT	AMOUNT USED	SAVED
RENT			
UTILITIES			
PHONE			
INSURANCE			
LOAN PAYMENTS			
GROCERIES			
DINING OUT			
TRANSPORTATION			
ENTERTAINMENT			
PERSONAL CARE			
HEALTH			
EMERGENCY FUND			
DONATIONS			
SUBSCRIPTIONS			
HOBBIES			
VACATIONS			
INVESTMENTS			

TOTAL INCOME	
TOTAL EXPENSES	
NET SAVINGS	

MONTHLY BUDGET

MONTH OF:

FIXED INCOME	
SIDE HUSTLE	
OTHER	
TOTAL INCOME	

CATEGORY	AMOUNT	AMOUNT USED	SAVED
RENT			
UTILITIES			
PHONE			
INSURANCE			
LOAN PAYMENTS			
GROCERIES			
DINING OUT			
TRANSPORTATION			
ENTERTAINMENT			
PERSONAL CARE			
HEALTH			
EMERGENCY FUND			
DONATIONS			
SUBSCRIPTIONS			
HOBBIES			
VACATIONS			
INVESTMENTS			

TOTAL INCOME	
TOTAL EXPENSES	
NET SAVINGS	

MONTHLY BUDGET

MONTH OF:

FIXED INCOME	
SIDE HUSTLE	
OTHER	
TOTAL INCOME	

CATEGORY	AMOUNT	AMOUNT USED	SAVED
RENT			
UTILITIES			
PHONE			
INSURANCE			
LOAN PAYMENTS			
GROCERIES			
DINING OUT			
TRANSPORTATION			
ENTERTAINMENT			
PERSONAL CARE			
HEALTH			
EMERGENCY FUND			
DONATIONS			
SUBSCRIPTIONS			
HOBBIES			
VACATIONS			
INVESTMENTS			

TOTAL INCOME	
TOTAL EXPENSES	
NET SAVINGS	

MONTHLY BUDGET

MONTH OF:

FIXED INCOME	
SIDE HUSTLE	
OTHER	
TOTAL INCOME	

CATEGORY	AMOUNT	AMOUNT USED	SAVED
RENT			
UTILITIES			
PHONE			
INSURANCE			
LOAN PAYMENTS			
GROCERIES			
DINING OUT			
TRANSPORTATION			
ENTERTAINMENT			
PERSONAL CARE			
HEALTH			
EMERGENCY FUND			
DONATIONS			
SUBSCRIPTIONS			
HOBBIES			
VACATIONS			
INVESTMENTS			

TOTAL INCOME	
TOTAL EXPENSES	
NET SAVINGS	

MONTHLY BUDGET

MONTH OF:

FIXED INCOME	
SIDE HUSTLE	
OTHER	
TOTAL INCOME	

CATEGORY	AMOUNT	AMOUNT USED	SAVED
RENT			
UTILITIES			
PHONE			
INSURANCE			
LOAN PAYMENTS			
GROCERIES			
DINING OUT			
TRANSPORTATION			
ENTERTAINMENT			
PERSONAL CARE			
HEALTH			
EMERGENCY FUND			
DONATIONS			
SUBSCRIPTIONS			
HOBBIES			
VACATIONS			
INVESTMENTS			

TOTAL INCOME	
TOTAL EXPENSES	
NET SAVINGS	

Financial Harmony

Days 71-75   Date: _____

Practice daily gratitude for the simplest financial blessings.

TODAY WE'RE GRATEFUL FOR

1	2	3

THINGS THAT MADE US SMILE TODAY

☺ _____

☺ _____

☺ _____

SOMETHING THAT INSPIRED US TODAY

PEOPLE WE'RE GRATEFUL TO HAVE IN OUR LIVES

Daily Affirmation:

_____

_____

NOTES & FREE THOUGHTS

Financial Harmony

Days 71-75

71-75

Date: _____

Practice daily gratitude for the simplest financial blessings.

TODAY WE'RE GRATEFUL FOR

1. _____
   _____

2. _____
   _____

3. _____
   _____

THINGS THAT MADE US SMILE TODAY

☺ _____

☺ _____

☺ _____

SOMETHING THAT INSPIRED US TODAY

PEOPLE WE'RE GRATEFUL TO HAVE IN OUR LIVES

Daily Affirmation:

_____

_____

NOTES & FREE THOUGHTS

Financial Harmony

Days 71-75

Date: _____

Practice daily gratitude for the simplest financial blessings.

TODAY WE'RE GRATEFUL FOR

1	2	3
_____	_____	_____
_____	_____	_____
_____	_____	_____

THINGS THAT MADE US SMILE TODAY

☺ _____

☺ _____

☺ _____

SOMETHING THAT INSPIRED US TODAY

PEOPLE WE'RE GRATEFUL TO HAVE IN OUR LIVES

Daily Affirmation:

_____

_____

NOTES & FREE THOUGHTS

Financial Harmony

Days 71-75 71-75

Date: _____

Practice daily gratitude for the simplest financial blessings.

TODAY WE'RE GRATEFUL FOR

1	2	3

THINGS THAT MADE US SMILE TODAY

☺ _____

☺ _____

☺ _____

SOMETHING THAT INSPIRED US TODAY

PEOPLE WE'RE GRATEFUL TO HAVE IN OUR LIVES

Daily Affirmation: _____

_____

NOTES & FREE THOUGHTS

Financial Harmony

Days 71-75

Date: _____

Practice daily gratitude for the simplest financial blessings.

TODAY WE'RE GRATEFUL FOR

1	2	3
_____	_____	_____
_____	_____	_____
_____	_____	_____

THINGS THAT MADE US SMILE TODAY

☺ _____

☺ _____

☺ _____

SOMETHING THAT INSPIRED US TODAY

PEOPLE WE'RE GRATEFUL TO HAVE IN OUR LIVES

Daily Affirmation:

_____

_____

NOTES & FREE THOUGHTS

Financial Harmony

Days 76-80   Date: _____

Research a new financial strategy, discuss, and plan its implementation.

STRATEGY WE TRIED:

_____
_____
_____
_____
_____
_____

RESULTS:

_____
_____
_____
_____
_____
_____

Financial Harmony

Days 76-80

76–80

Date: _____

Research a new financial strategy, discuss, and plan its implementation.

STRATEGY WE TRIED:

_____

_____

_____

_____

_____

_____

RESULTS:

_____

_____

_____

_____

_____

_____

Financial Harmony

Days 76-80

Date: _____

Research a new financial strategy, discuss, and plan its implementation.

STRATEGY WE TRIED:

_____
_____
_____
_____
_____

RESULTS:

_____
_____
_____
_____
_____

Financial Harmony

Days 76-80

Date: _____

Research a new financial strategy, discuss, and plan its implementation.

STRATEGY WE TRIED:

_____

_____

_____

_____

_____

RESULTS:

_____

_____

_____

_____

_____

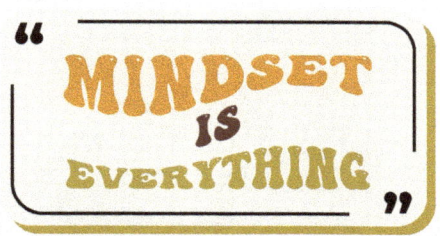

Financial Harmony

Days 76-80

Date: _____

Research a new financial strategy, discuss, and plan its implementation.

STRATEGY WE TRIED:

_____
_____
_____
_____
_____

RESULTS:

_____
_____
_____
_____
_____

Financial Harmony

Days 81-85 85

Date: _____

Commit to a no-spend challenge for a weekend and relish free activities.

FREE ACTIVITIES WE TRIED DURING
OUR NO-SPEND CHALLENGE:

1. _____
2. _____
3. _____
4. _____
5. _____
6. _____
7. _____
8. _____
9. _____
10. _____
11. _____
12. _____
13. _____
14. _____
15. _____

The *Future* depends on what you *Do Today*

Financial Harmony

Days 86-90   Date: _____

Share, discuss, and appreciate each other's individual financial goals.

1. _____
2. _____
3. _____
4. _____
5. _____
6. _____
7. _____
8. _____
9. _____
10. _____
11. _____
12. _____
13. _____
14. _____
15. _____
16. _____
17. _____
18. _____
19. _____
20. _____

Bonus Resources

REFLECTION & FUTURE PLANNING

Reflect on the journey, discuss what worked, and plan how to continue prioritizing your marriage.

REFLECTION & FUTURE PLANNING

Reflect on the journey, discuss what worked, and plan how to continue prioritizing your marriage.

_____
_____
_____
_____
_____
_____
_____
_____
_____
_____
_____
_____
_____
_____
_____
_____

REFLECTION & FUTURE PLANNING

Reflect on the journey, discuss what worked, and plan how to continue prioritizing your marriage.

REFLECTION & FUTURE PLANNING

Reflect on the journey, discuss what worked, and plan how to continue prioritizing your marriage.

REFLECTION & FUTURE PLANNING

Reflect on the journey, discuss what worked, and plan how to continue prioritizing your marriage.

INTIMACY MAINTENANCE CHECKLIST

Intimacy isn't an act but a loving commitment to your relationship. How did you nurture your marriage this week?

Date

- Take a long bath together
- Had a date night in
- Went for a walk together
- Prayed together
- Planned for our future
- Tried a new restaurant
- Cooked a meal together
- Cuddled on the couch
- Held hands
- Discussed our fears

Date

- Enjoyed a staycation
- Listened to music
- Spent quiet time together
- Watched a movie together
- Got a couples' massage
- Went on a road trip
- Had spontaneous sex
- Sent random love texts
- Tried a new class or activity
- Explored a new place

INTIMACY MAINTENANCE CHECKLIST

Use the spaces below to fill in your own intimacy activities.
Keep it spicy! 😉

Date

Date